CHURCH NEEDLEPOINT

Patterns and Instructions

Louise A. Raynor
and
Carolyn H. Kerr

MOREHOUSE-BARLOW COMPANY
Wilton, Connecticut

Dedicated to

The Cathedral Church of St. Paul

and

The Diocese of Vermont

©1976 Morehouse-Barlow Co., Inc.
78 Danbury Road
Wilton, Conn. 06897

SBN-0-8192-1214-8

Printed in the United States of America

Table of Contents

FOREWORD

This book of patterns and instructions grew out of a needlepoint project devised to provide kneelers for the Cathedral Church of St. Paul, Burlington, Vermont.

The first few kneeler canvases were bought with worked patterns, but soon after the project's inception Louise Raynor took over as designer. The designs were kept simple because all the preliminary layout and pattern working was to be done by only four persons. For the sake of uniformity in the finished work and because the canvases were to be worked by persons varying in experience and expertise, simple directions for the completion of the needlepoint were developed.

Carolyn Kerr directed the project and, with Sandy Herchenson, developed a method for mounting the completed needlepoint which made the kneelers suitable for use on St. Paul's slate floors.

With the kneeler project nearing completion, and with the work for the Cathedral a point of departure, this book was conceived. The patterns were reworked and many new ones added to the collection. The directions were expanded to include materials and mountings. Small motifs and borders were designed and various layouts devised to extend the use of the patterns to church furnishings other than individual kneelers.

It is the hope of the authors that this publication will help individuals and parishes develop needlepoint projects for their churches.

Louise Raynor and Carolyn Kerr

Burlington, Vermont
Eastertide 1976

INTRODUCTION

Needlepoint, as the term is used today,[1] is a form of canvas embroidery with very ancient roots. The exact place of its origin is not known although there is evidence of its production in Egypt and the Orient by the fourth century A.D.

Used in ecclesiastical work for centuries, needlepoint was combined with other forms of embroidery. Churches and cathedrals throughout England and Europe are noted for the beauty of their needlepoint articles. In some instances, the work is elaborate and intricate, with silk and metallic threads being used in addition to the usual wool.

While only expert needlewomen could produce pieces like those that survive in museums and in the treasuries of ancient cathedrals, over the years many women have become adept in the art in its simpler forms. Today, such work is very popular and is uniquely appropriate for church embellishment.

Designs and patterns found in ancient and modern works are basically of two kinds — pictorial and symbolic.[2] The two may be combined. Pictorial needlework ranges from the crude and naive to the highly realistic with scenes representing events from the Old and New Testaments abounding. However, a

---

[1]Accurately, the term "needlepoint" refers to a type of handmade lace and what, today, is called needlepoint should be referred to as a type of canvas embroidery.

[2]See pages 6 and 8.

KING DAVID. Top of seat cushion from Washington Cathedral. This beautiful and complex piece of needlepoint is presented to show the spaces on either side of a circular design filled with ancient musical instruments. (Reprinted by permission of The Cathedral of Sts. Peter and Paul, Washington, D.C.)

large proportion of needlepoint work involves symbolism. The earliest Christian communities used symbols to represent persons and events and to convey simple ideas. One source from which they drew was the symbolic language of the Bible. A second origin for symbols is to be found in well known objects as used, for example, in trade and capital punishment — the carpenter's square, the ship, the balance, stones, and the sword. Such objects were combined to stand for apostle, saint, and martyr. Nature, too, was drawn upon to represent certain attributes. For example, the lily came to symbolize purity,[3] the oak to stand for faith and endurance, the lion to portray courage. For examples of both pictorial and symbolic needlepoint pieces, see pages 6 and 8.

The representation of both pictorial and symbolic patterns in all the graphic arts, including needlepoint, involves, much of the time, the use of color. Color has developed its own symbolism over the years. For example, red stands for martyrdom, blue for heavenly love, white for holiness and innocence. An account of the significance of colors, as well as the meaning ascribed to certain objects, plants, and animals may be found in W. Ellwood Post's *Saints, Signs and Symbols.* (For information see page 71.) Color has been used extensively in cathedrals and churches, partly in a symbolic manner, partly for purely artistic decoration. Color is found built into the fabric of the buildings, in windows, frescoes, and mosaics, it is used extensively also in vestments, hangings, kneelers, and cushions. The latter articles are most suitable as subjects for present-day needlepoint work.

In the development of needlepoint patterns, there are two very different approaches. In one approach, the design is worked up very much as for a painting with little regard, if any, for the structure of the needlepoint canvas and thread count. For designs of naturalistic animal and vegetable life this method can be very satisfactory. For precise forms and geometric structures, however, it leaves much to be desired. For these latter subjects, the careful plotting of the pattern, stitch by stitch, on graph paper produces a more refined design. For the best results, patterns of this kind should be constructed on paper

[3]The lily, or fleur-de-lys, is used as a symbol for the Virgin Mary.

lined to give ten spaces to the inch in both directions, with the inches marked with heavier lines to help in the counting. This method is used in all of the patterns in this publication. For a series of pictures and diagrams illustrating the process see page 19.

The patterns presented in this book — numbering thirty-eight in all — are limited to the symbolic representation of the evangelists, the apostles, a few other important saints, plus symbols for the seasons and feast days of the Christian Year, and a selection of crosses. A detailed listing of the patterns is to be found on page 24.

The designs are suitable for single kneelers or they may be used in a variety of other ways which are dealt with in the section on *Suggested Layouts,* page 11. A section on *Color and Wool,* page 15, and a treatment of *Stitches and Canvas,* page 18, precede the *Patterns* section, page 24. The book closes with an illustrated section on *Blocking and Mounting* beginning on page 65.

FLEUR-DE-LYS AND MONOGRAM. This kneeler top — used in the Washington Cathedral — has an overall design combining the fleur-de-lys and the monogram of the Virgin Mary. (Reprinted by permission of the Cathedral of Sts. Peter and Paul, Washington, D.C.)

PRELIMINARY DIRECTIONS

CANVAS for needlepoint comes in two basic types: a single thread mesh known as *MONO* and a double thread mesh called *PENELOPE.* In Penelope, the threads running up and down the canvas, as the canvas comes from the roll, are more closely paired than those running across, but spacing is such that ten stitches cover the same distance in both directions.

Canvas is described by referring to the number of meshes or holes per inch. Thus, No. 10 canvas has ten meshes or holes per inch. No. 10 is very satisfactory to work with, although finer and coarser canvas is available. It comes in several widths and can be purchased by the yard.

Before the amount of canvas to buy can be determined, it must be decided whether only the top of a cushion is to be worked in needlepoint, or if the sides are to be worked as well. When a cushion is rectangular, consider working the top and the attached sides and, after sewing the corners, adding a non-needlepoint back. With any tapered or rounded cushion, work only the top in needlepoint and have the piece boxed with a band of velveteen around the sides. While thickness is a matter of choice, no less than two inches — when finished — is suggested and two and one-half to three inches may be better in some situations. See the sections on *Blocking and Mounting,* page 65, for detailed directions.

When calculating the amount of canvas to buy, figure four to five inches extra all around the area to be worked, to allow for handling, blocking, and finishing. Cut edges should be bound with masking tape or turned over half an inch and stitched on the sewing machine.

WOOL for needlepoint is discussed in detail in the section on *Colors and Wool,* page 15. It is best to use light-resistant, mothproof, matched dye lot tapestry yarn or the three-stranded Persian type wool. When No. 10 canvas is used and *continental* and *diagonal tent* stitches, one yard of wool is required for each square inch of canvas. Before starting, buy the necessary amount of yarn to complete the project to make sure that all yarn is from the same dye lot.

NEEDLES used in canvas embroidery should be smooth and blunt, the so called *tapestry needles*. Usually, work on No. 10 canvas can be done best with a No. 18 or a No. 20 needle. When threaded, the needle should pull easily through the mesh, with no tendency to spread it.

SUGGESTED LAYOUTS

The thirty-eight patterns in this collection may be used in many ways. A few are presented in Plate 1 on page 12. While these diagrams show only patterns within rectangles, they may be used within any shape desired. None of the layouts is shown with attached sides, but, for most cushions, it is well to extend the needlepoint thus:

By doing this, a great deal of fussy assembling is eliminated.

Regardless of the way you use any design, plan the layout, measure, count meshes, and calculate very carefully. Use graph paper (10 lines per inch suggested) when you lay out more complicated pieces and, always, count the square for accuracy of spacing.

The thirty-eight patterns as diagrammed are suitable for a twelve by fifteen inch, one-person kneeler, with or without a border added. See Plate 1, Fig. 1. Possible border designs and small decorative units are shown on Plate 2, on page 14. To use the patterns on larger cushions, or in other ways, many modifications may be made. Continuing to refer to Plate 1:

Borders may be modified either by being made narrower, Fig. 2, or wider, Fig. 6. They may be moved in from the edge to break the space better, Fig. 5, or omitted entirely, Fig. 4.

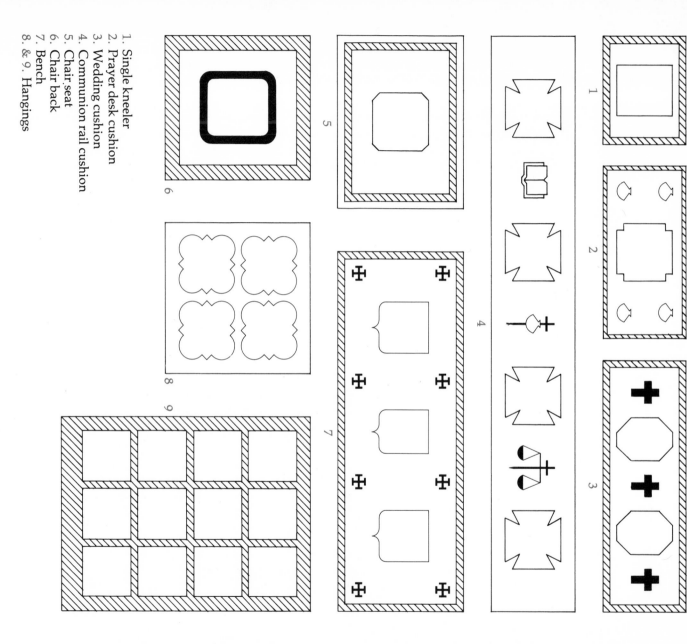

1. Single kneeler
2. Prayer desk cushion
3. Wedding cushion
4. Communion rail cushion
5. Chair seat
6. Chair back
7. Bench
8. & 9. Hangings

Plate 1 — *SUGGESTED LAYOUTS*

Small Units — crosses, shells, *etc.* — (see Plate 2) can be used to break the background area in a prayer desk kneeler, wedding cushion, or bench seat. See Plate 1. Figs. 2, 3, and 7.

Framing of the pattern may be modified, that is, made wider or larger, Fig. 6, or the shape changed.

Unframed patterns may be used if preferred, alone on a small kneeler, or in combination with framed patterns, as in a communion rail cushion, Fig. 4.

Portions of many of the patterns can provide small decorative units: the sword, the book, the shell, or the central part of a cross.

Grouping evangelists, apostles, or seasons of the Christian Year, is suggested for hangings. See Figs. 8 and 9.

Color changes can do much to add interest and variety. Tradition, need not be followed, nor is uniformity always desirable within the same or closely related pieces of needlepoint.

SEDILIA cushion, St. James Church, Arlington, Vermont. The illustration here shows but one of the three. The escallop (or scallop) shell, one of the symbols of St. James the Greater, was used to break the space between shield and border.

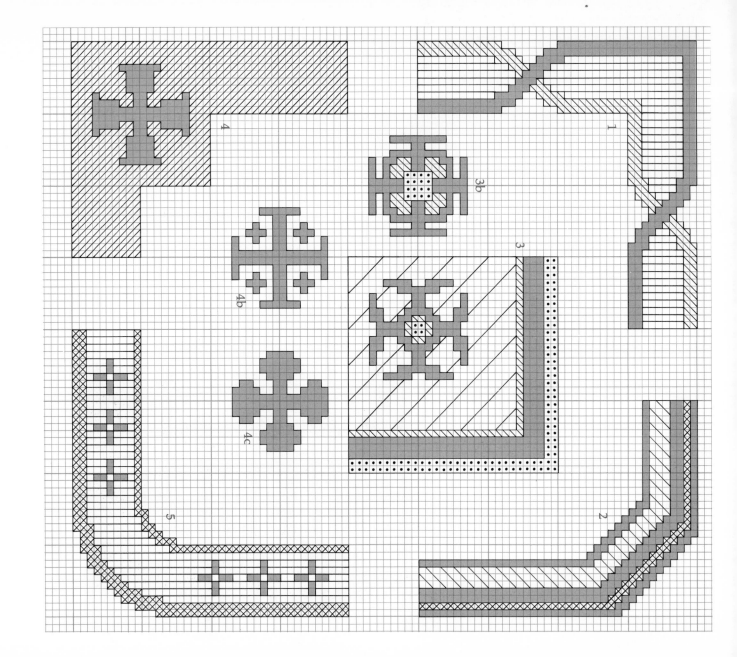

COLORS AND WOOL

In the choice of colors, at least four questions — all of which are important — must be considered:

1. In what kind of *setting* is the needlepoint to be used — traditional or modern, dark or bright, colorful or colorless?

2. In what type of *light* will it be viewed? Some lighting can change completely the appearance of yarn color.

3. Are there *symbolic* or *traditional* colors which should be incorporated into the pattern? Here, the particular shades of the colors selected can change the whole tone of the needlepoint piece.

4. Your own *personal preference* should be taken into account. Before starting, get samples of your colors and look at them together in the place where the needlepoint is to be placed. Too much time and expense is involved for you not to be sure exactly what is best.

COLORS are indicated on the thirty-eight patterns presented.

Traditional colors are given where there is an established symbolism, as for the apostles. However, they do not have to be used.

Suggested colors are listed in other cases. If these do not suit your situation or taste, change them.

Color for the **Outlines** of the shields, or other pattern shapes, are not indicated. Black, Gold, or Silver are used frequently. The choice should relate to the colors in the pattern and to general background colors.

When **Borders** are used, they should be worked in colors which appear in or relate to the main pattern.

WOOL COLORS are presented in the table on page 17. Lady Handicraft and Bucilla yarns are listed. They are suitable for use on No. 10 canvas. "Lady Handicraft Needlepoint Yarn" comes in forty yard skeins. A good tapestry wool, it is a light-resistant, matched dye lot, four-ply, single-strand yarn and is easy to work with. The Bucilla yarn is a "Needlepoint and Crewel Wool," of the Persian type, which comes ten yards to the card or in ten-yard skeins. This wool is three-stranded, each strand being two-ply. It is silicone treated and more glossy than the tapestry wool. Neither brand provides all colors and both make many other colors. While we recommend these two yarns, there is no reason for not using other reliable makes of needlepoint yarn which may be available. **Do not use knitting wool.** Always figure on one yard of either type wool to work one square inch on No. 10 canvas when using the *continental* and *diagonal tent* stitches. See pages 19 and 21.

WOOL, if not available where you live, may be obtained by ordering from The Yarn Cellar, 96 Church Street, Burlington, Vermont 05401. (It would be well to mention that you obtained their address from this publication.) The distributor of the British made Lady Handicraft is Columbia-Minerva Corp. The American made Bucilla yarn is manufactured by Berngard Ulmann Co.

TABLE OF COLORS AND WOOLS

COLOR		LADY HANDICRAFT	BUCILLA
VIOLET	Reddish		31
	Bluish		72
BLUE	Deep	French	420 T
	Medium	Gobelin	419 T
	Bright	Powder	417 T
	Light	Bluebird	465 / 43
	Very Light	Light Blue	464 / 33
	Aqua	Azure	408 T
GREEN	Deep	Loden	476
	Medium	Avocado	479 / 8
	Olive	Olive	478
	Yellowish	Lettuce	481
GOLD	Dark	Gold Nugget	460
	Medium	Regency Gold	402 T
		Pastel Gold	456
	Bright	Goldenrod	482 / 3
	Light	Marigold	470 / 116
ORANGE			94
RED	Deep	Regency Red	448 T / 36
	Bright	Scarlet	474 / 35
BLACK			423 / 12
GRAY	Dark		108
	Medium		107
	Silver		106
WHITE	Ivory	Ivory	435 T
	Wool	Snow	463
	Bright	Glamour	477 / 1
BROWN		Chestnut	421 / 41
FLESH	Medium	Dusty Rose	410 T
		Rose Beige	449
	Light	Peony Pink	468
		Cream	425 T

STITCHES AND CANVAS

STITCHES recommended for church needlepoint are selected to give a compact, strong, well-wearing fabric. For lines use the *continental* stitch; for areas use the *diagonal tent* stitch.

CANVAS of either of two types may be used: Penelope or Mono. With the Penelope, each stitch covers the intersection of two pairs of threads; with Mono canvas, each stitch covers a single crossing.

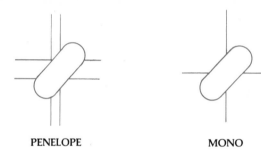

PENELOPE   MONO

TERMS used in the stitch diagrams and their explanations follow:

Front - side to be mounted outward in finished work
Back - underside
North- top edge, front of work
South- bottom edge, front of work
East - right edge, front of work
West - left edge, front of work

> When the words "top" and "right" are used confusion results.

Continental Stitch
for lines

ON PENELOPE

ON MONO

NORTH

WEST

EAST

SOUTH

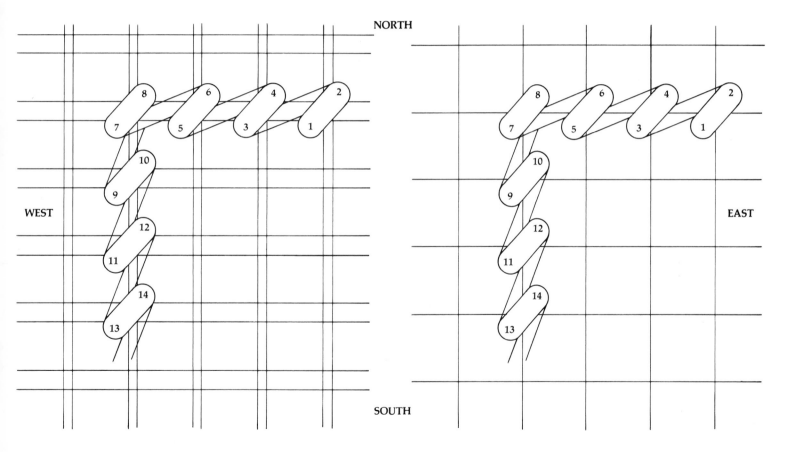

CONTINENTAL STITCH must always be worked East to West or North to South. **Note** — the wool on the front side of the canvas **always** runs SW to NE. This holds for all stitches on the canvas.

> **From back,** first bring needle through at 1. In subsequent stitches, bring the needle through at all odd numbers. Hold an inch or so of the wool on the back and work over it as you progress, or run new thread into the back of a finished area.

> **On front,** slant the wool NE over intersection of threads and insert needle at 2. In all subsequent stitches, insert needle at even numbers.

> **On back,** pass needle under two intersections thus:

ON PENELOPE

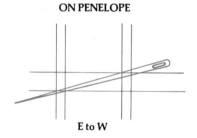

E to W

ON MONO

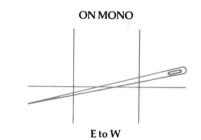

E to W

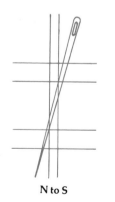

N to S

N to S

Diagonal Tent Stitch

for areas

ON PENELOPE

ON MONO

NORTH

WEST

EAST

SOUTH

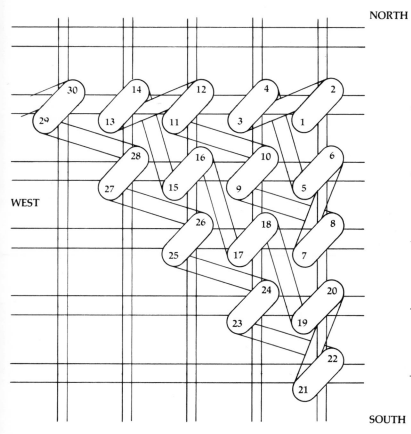

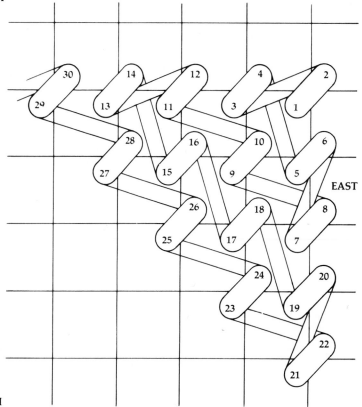

DIAGONAL TENT STITCH is worked on the slant. NW to SE rows alternate with SE to NW rows. Work should always start at the NE corner. On the back, a basket weave appearance develops.

From back, bring the needle through at 1. In subsequent stitches, bring needle through at all odd numbers. Hold an inch or so of the wool on the back and work over it as you progress, or run new thread into back of finished area.

On the front, slant the wool NE over one intersection of threads and insert needle at 2. In all subsequent stitches insert needle at even numbers. Throughout the canvas all stitches should slant this way.

On the back, as in Continental Stitch, the length of thread per stitch is greater than on the front, its direction and reinsertion varies as follows:

On NW to SE rows the needle is pointed approximately SOUTH and passes under 2 threads or 2 pairs of threads. (See below.)

On SE to NW rows the needle is pointed approximately WEST and passes under 2 threads, or 2 pairs of threads. (See below.)

ON PENELOPE

ON MONO

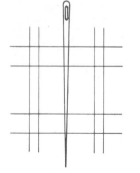

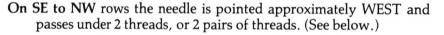

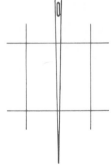

NW to SE

SE to NW

SE to NW

NW to SE

Reversal of Direction takes place along North and East lines. Here you are actually taking a Continental Stitch. Along the North edge as in a horizontal line of Continental Stitches, along the East as in a vertical line. See diagram for Continental Stitch, page 19.

WASHINGTON CATHEDRAL STAFF here reproduced, in stylized fashion, on two corridor bench cushions. This pictures a most interesting way in which a number of figures can be combined, with the use of a series of arches, into a united composition. Notice the way these cushions had to be shaped especially to fit the stonework and that the designs were fashioned most carefully to conform to the cushion shapes. (Reprinted by permission of the Cathedral of Sts. Peter and Paul, Washington, D.C.)

PATTERNS

The thirty-eight patterns of this book represent the evangelists, the apostles and a few other important saints, the seasons and festivals of the Christian Year, and a selection of crosses. In most instances, the patterns are based on traditional symbols which can be found in such publications as are listed in the References, page 71. A listing and the sequence in which they are arranged follow.

The patterns which follow were drawn on graph paper with each small square representing one stitch and one-tenth of an inch. The graph paper has heavier lines every ten spaces, marking off ten stitches, or one inch. This aids in the counting and in calculating size. In every case, the center of the design is placed in the exact center of the graph paper, where two heavy lines intersect. This is to facilitate centering the pattern on the canvas. All the patterns represent an area approximately eight by eight inches in size. (Please note — the patterns in this book have been reduced 25%.) In many cases, the outline frames can be interchanged if it seems desirable.

Since expense prohibits printing the patterns in color, the colors are coded. Assorted cross hatching, x's, *etc.*, are used to indicate individual colors. There is no uniformity in this coding, from one pattern to another. While, for example, red is not always marked in the same way, symbols are used in such a way as to make the various parts of any pattern clearly distinguishable. It is suggested that, when one of the involved patterns is used, the worker add color to the pattern to make it easier to follow.

SAINTS AND SEASONS OF THE CHURCH — NEEDLEPOINT PATTERNS

Suggested Colors

Face and Hands —
  ⊙ Light Flesh
Neck —
  ◉ Medium Flesh
Scroll —
  ⊞ Ivory or White
Robe —
  ⊠ Medium and
  ☐ Deep Blue
Wings —
  ◹ Silver
  ◿ Medium Gray

Frame: Ivory

Background:
  Very Light Blue

IMPORTANT — Plan balance
of shades carefully so none
will be too dark or too pale,
yet the pattern will be clear.

1. St. Matthew — Evangelist

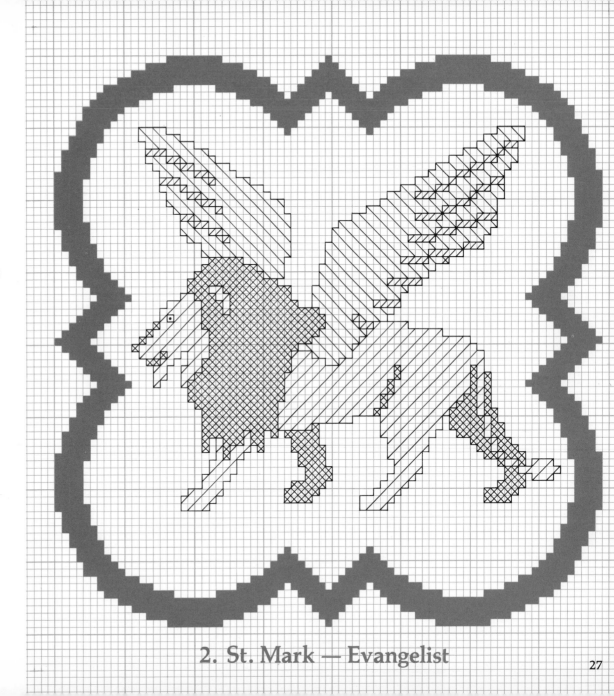

Suggested Colors

Lion:

  Body —
- ☑ Light Gold
- ☒ Deep Gold

  Wings —
- ◨ Silver
- ▨ Medium Gray

  Eye —
- ⊡ Black with a French knot of white sewing silk for highlight added after completion of needlepoint.

Frame: Ivory

Background:
  Medium Blue

2. St. Mark — Evangelist

Suggested Colors

Ox:

Body —
⊠ ☑ Shades of Gold or Brown

Horns, muzzle, and hooves —
◼ Black

Wings —
◻ Silver
☑ Medium Gray

Eye —
⊡ Black with a French knot of white sewing silk for highlight. Add after needlepoint is completed.

Frame: Ivory

Background: Medium Blue

3. St. Luke — Evangelist

Suggested Colors

Eagle:

Body — Regency Gold

Wings and Tail —
☑ Goldenrod
▨ Gold Nugget

Beak and Perch —
⊠ Silver

Claws and Eye —
⊠ ⊡ Black

Add French knot of white sewing silk for highlight.

Frame: Ivory

Background:
Medium Blue

4. St. John — Evangelist

29

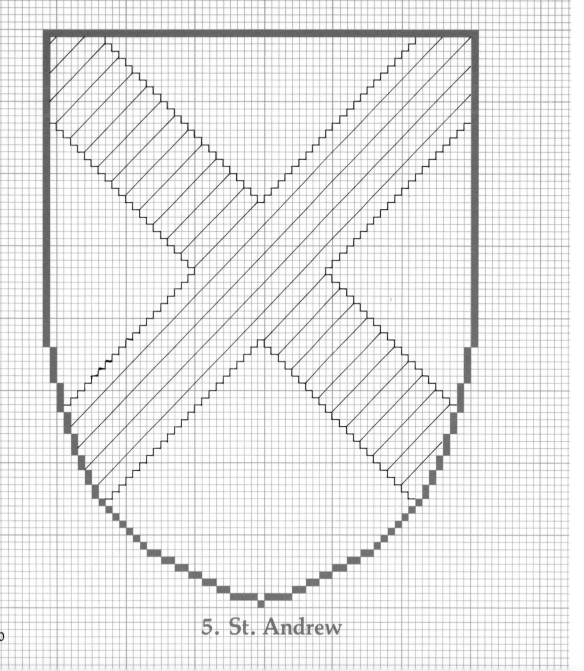

5. St. Andrew

Suggested Colors

Traditional Colors:

Cross:
  ☑ Silver

Shield: Deep Blue

Frame:
  Ivory or your choice.

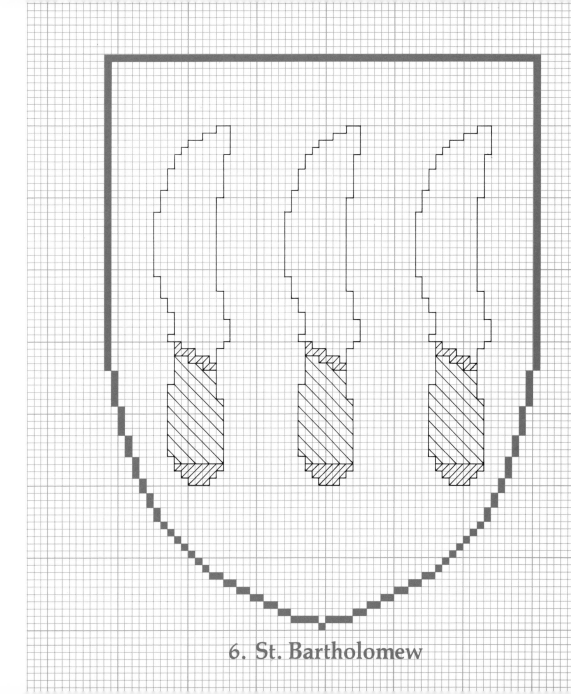

Suggested Colors

Traditional Colors:

Knives:

Blades — Silver

Handles —

◻ Goldenrod

◻ Gold Nugget

Shield: Scarlet

Frame: Ivory, White, or your choice.

6. St. Bartholomew

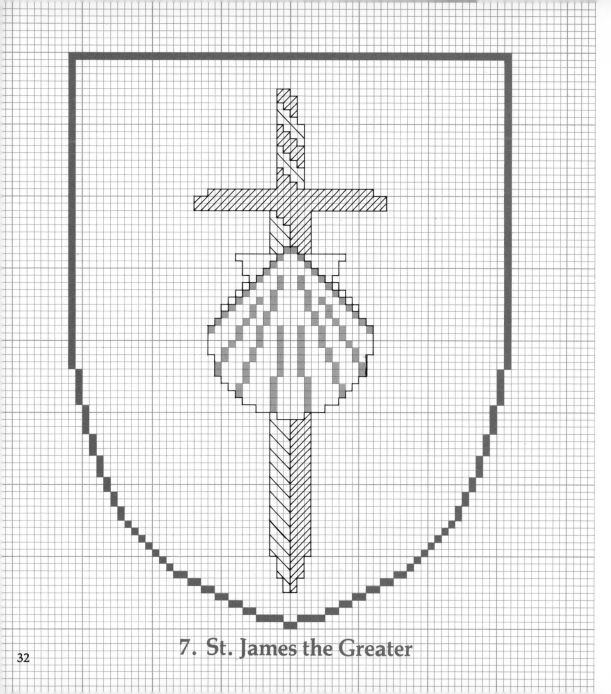

7. St. James the Greater

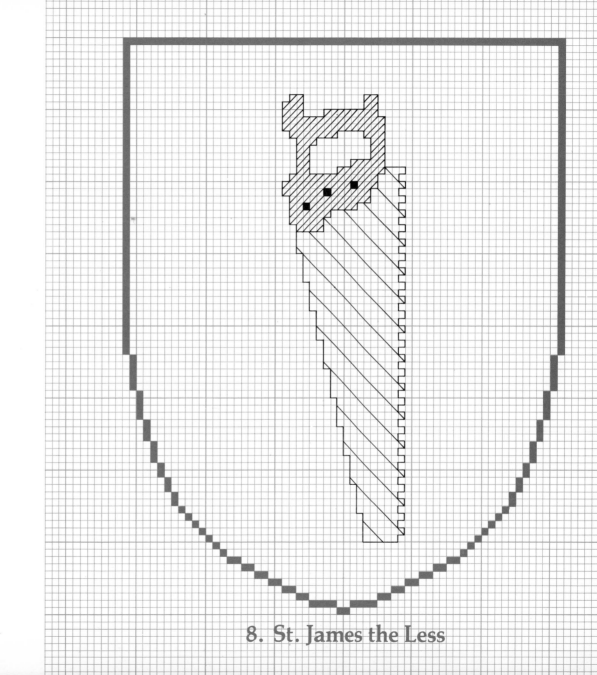

Suggested Colors

Traditional Colors:

Saw:

    Handle —

        ☑ Goldenrod

    Screws —

        ■ Black

    Blade —

        ◩ Silver

Shield: Scarlet

Frame: Ivory, White, or
    your choice.

8. St. James the Less

33

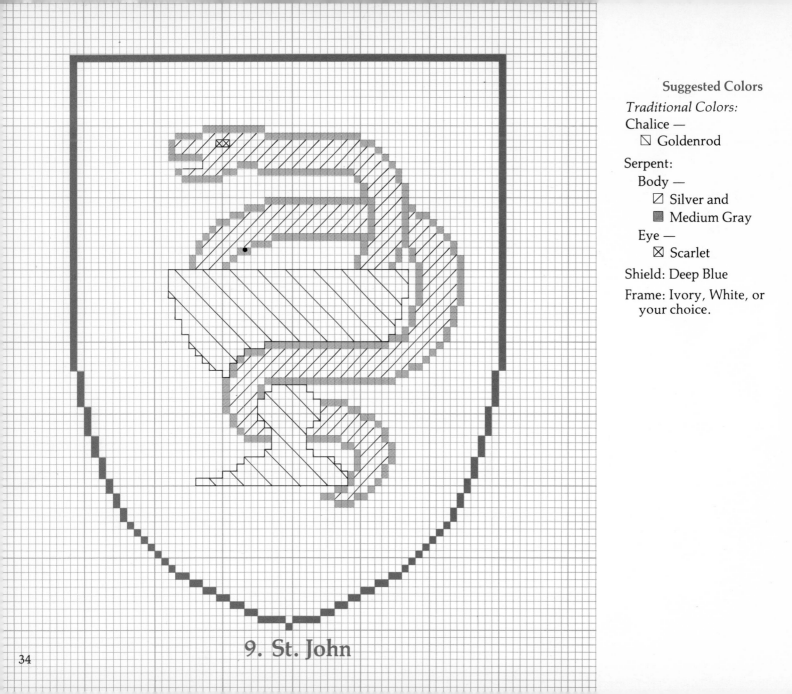

Suggested Colors

Traditional Colors:

Chalice —
  ◨ Goldenrod

Serpent:
  Body —
    ◪ Silver and
    ■ Medium Gray
  Eye —
    ⊠ Scarlet

Shield: Deep Blue

Frame: Ivory, White, or
  your choice.

9. St. John

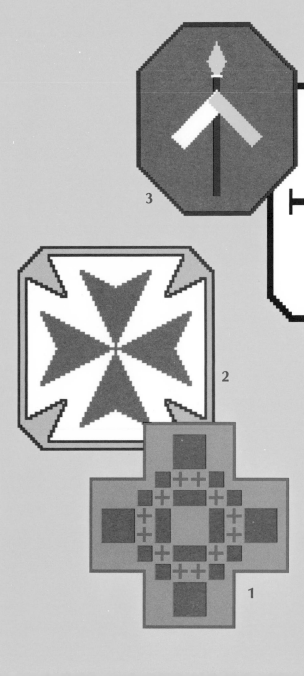

1. Apostles Cross (page 60)
2. St. John the Baptist (page 45)
3. St. Thomas (page 41)
4. Evangelists' Cross (page 63)
5. Easter-Resurrection (page 52)

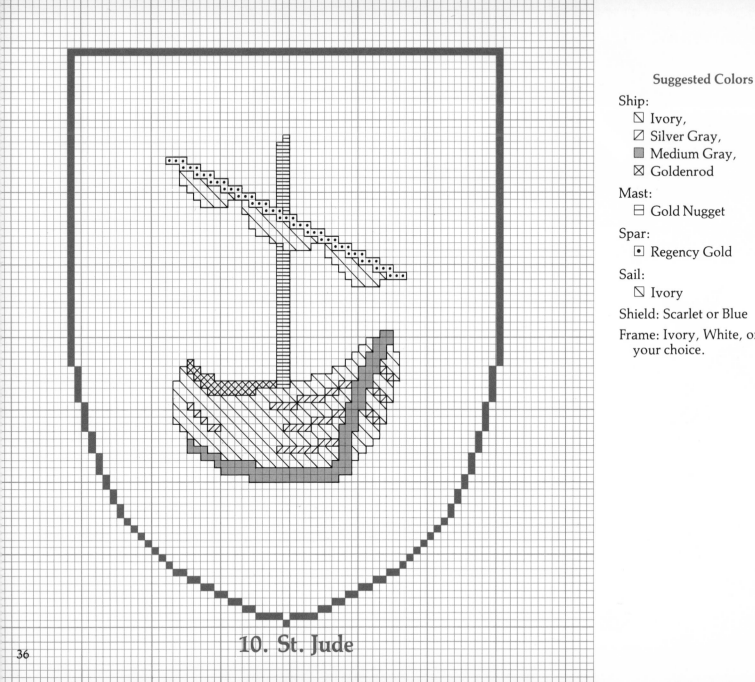

Suggested Colors

Ship:
◤ Ivory,
◩ Silver Gray,
▩ Medium Gray,
⊠ Goldenrod

Mast:
⊟ Gold Nugget

Spar:
⊡ Regency Gold

Sail:
◤ Ivory

Shield: Scarlet or Blue

Frame: Ivory, White, or your choice.

10. St. Jude

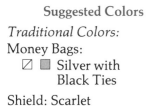
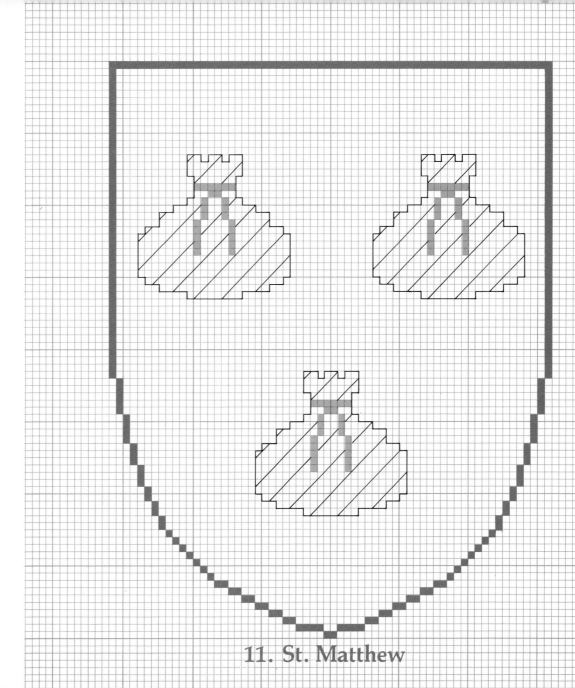

11. St. Matthew

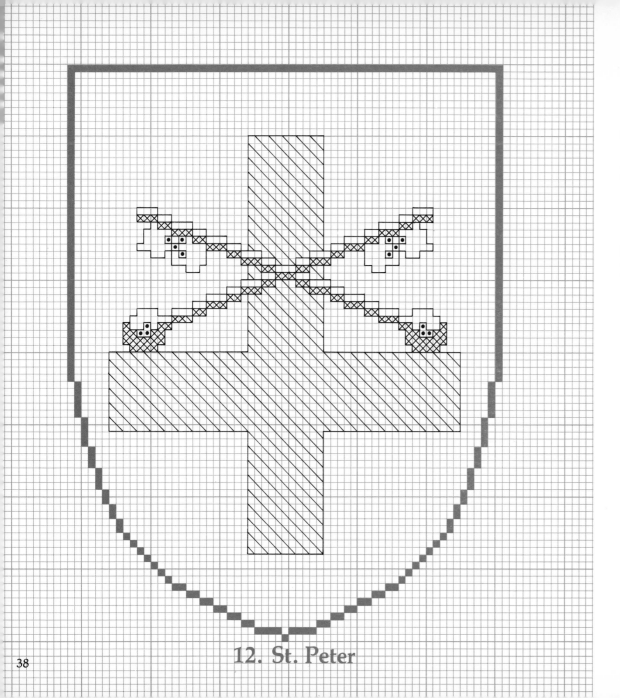

12. St. Peter

Suggested Colors

Traditional Colors:

Cross:
  ◨ Black

Keys:
  ☐ Silver,
  ⊠ Medium Gray,
  ⊡ Scarlet

Shield: Scarlet

Frame: White, Ivory, or your choice.

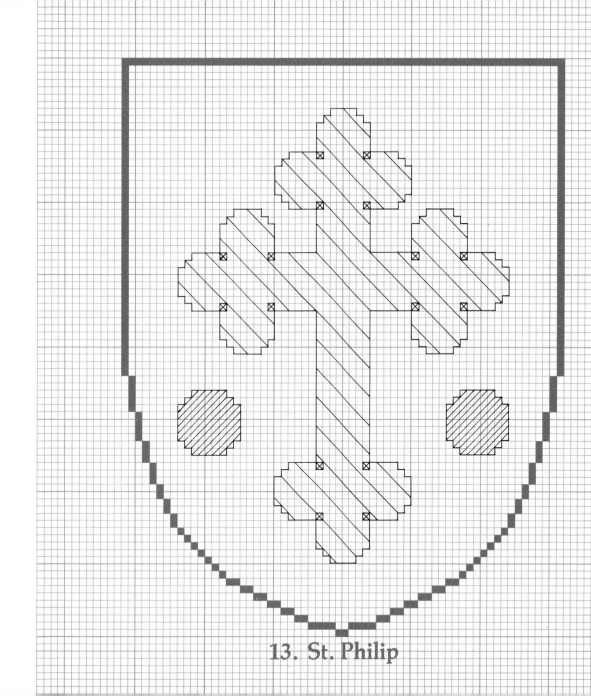

Suggested Colors

Traditional Colors:

Cross:
  ◩ Goldenrod
  ☒ Scarlet

Roundels:
  ◨ Silver

Shield: Scarlet

Frame: White, Ivory, or
  your choice.

13. St. Philip

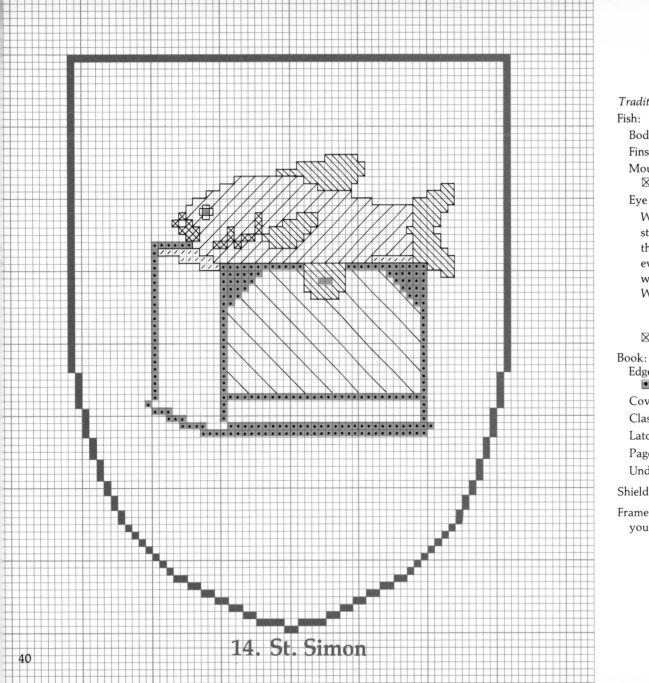

14. St. Simon

Suggested Colors

Traditional Colors:

Fish:

    Body — ☑ Silver

    Fins — ◹ Medium Gray

    Mouth and Gill —
        ⊠ Dark Gray

    Eye —

        Work in petit point. The 2 x 2
        stitch area should have canvas
        threads respaced to give an
        even 4 x 4 mesh. Then, use
        wool split to half thickness.
        Work thus —

        ⊠ Black, • White, ☐ Silver

Book:

    Edges, Corners, etc. —
        ◉ Gold Nugget

    Cover — ◹ Goldenrod

    Clasp — ◹ Medium Gray

    Latch — ■ Black

    Pages — ☐ White

    Under fish — ☑ Light Gold

Shield: Scarlet

Frame: White, Ivory, or
   your choice

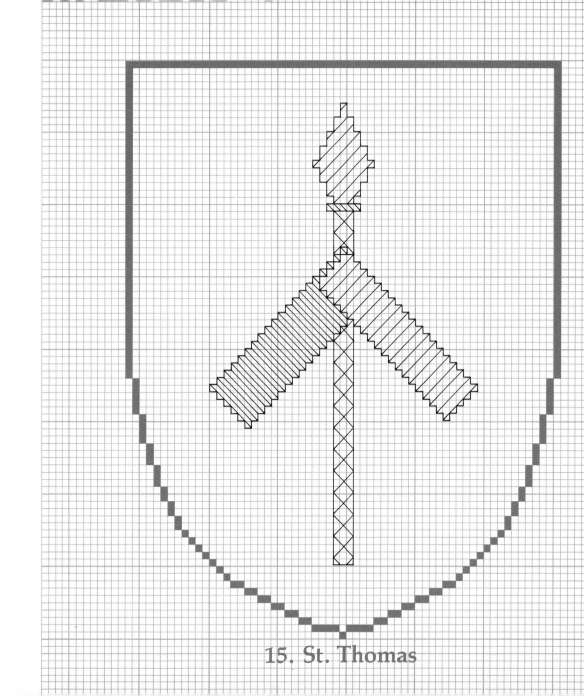

Suggested Colors

Traditional Colors:

Carpenter's Square:
- ☑ Silver
- ◨ Goldenrod

Spear:
- Head —
  - ☑ Silver
- Band —
  - ◨ Goldenrod
- Handle —
  - ⊠ Gold Nugget

Shield: Scarlet

Frame: White, Ivory, or your choice

15. St. Thomas

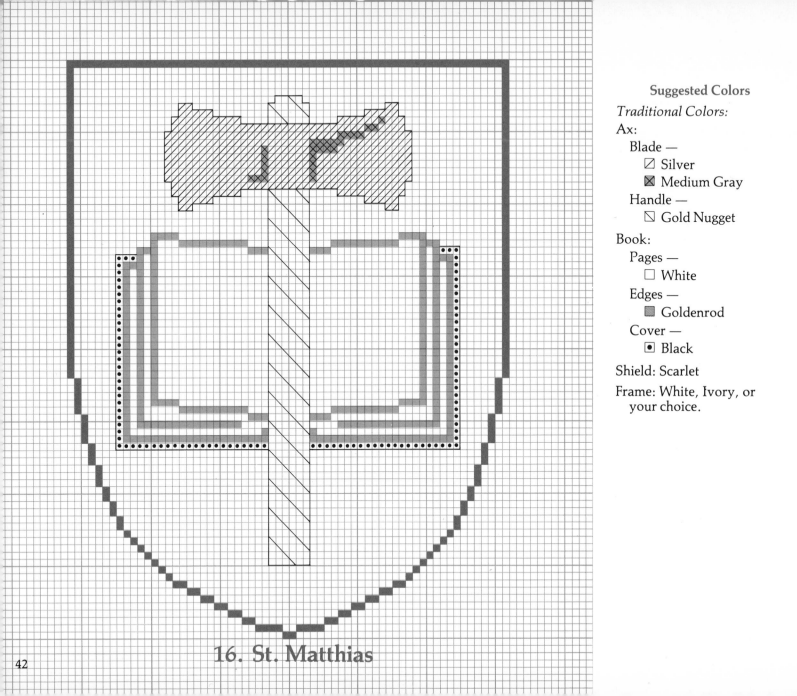

Traditional Colors:

Ax:

    Blade —

        ☑ Silver

        ☒ Medium Gray

    Handle —

        ◨ Gold Nugget

Book:

    Pages —

        ☐ White

    Edges —

        ▨ Goldenrod

    Cover —

        ⊡ Black

Shield: Scarlet

Frame: White, Ivory, or your choice.

16. St. Matthias

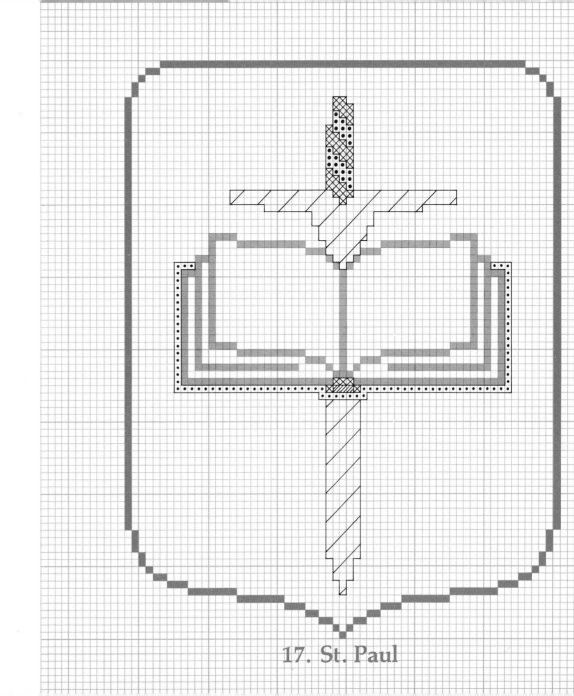

Suggested Colors

Sword:
- ☑ Silver
- ☒ Gold Nugget
- ◉ Goldenrod

Book:
  Pages —
  - ☐ Ivory, outlined in
  - ▨ Regency Gold

  Cover —
  - ◉ Black
  - ☑ Dark Gray

  Cording —
  - ☒ Deep Blue

Shield: Scarlet

Frame: White, Ivory, or your choice.

17. St. Paul

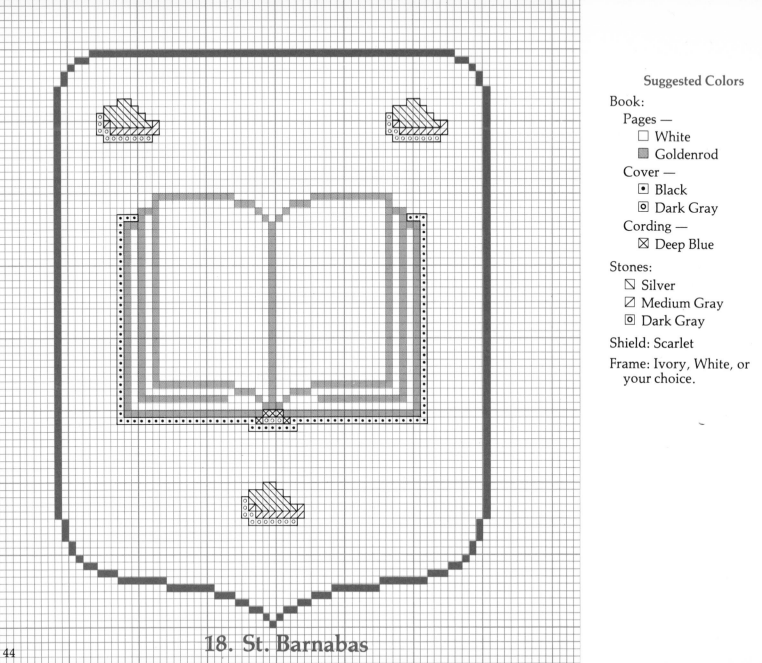

Book:
  Pages —
    ☐ White
    ▣ Goldenrod
  Cover —
    ⊡ Black
    ◉ Dark Gray
  Cording —
    ⊠ Deep Blue

Stones:
  ◻ Silver
  ◺ Medium Gray
  ◉ Dark Gray

Shield: Scarlet

Frame: Ivory, White, or your choice.

18. St. Barnabas

Suggested Colors

Maltese Cross:
☑ Scarlet

Borders:
▣ French Blue

Border fill-in:
◳ Regency Gold

Background: White

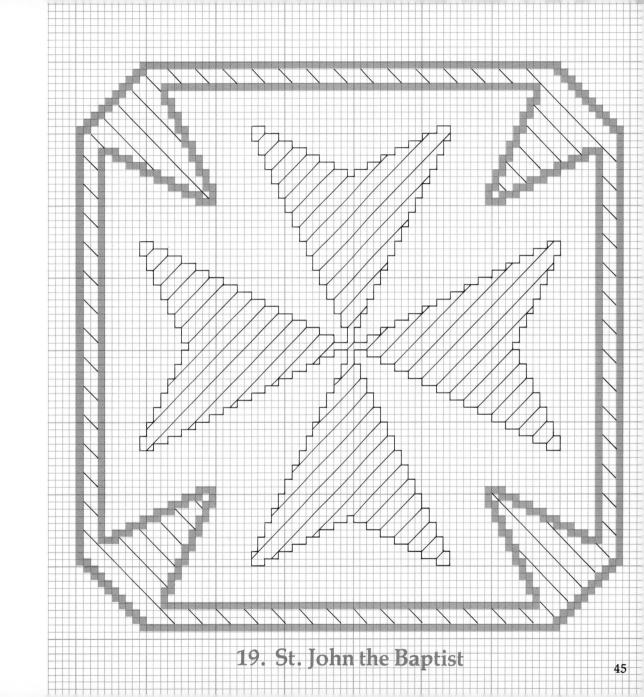

19. St. John the Baptist

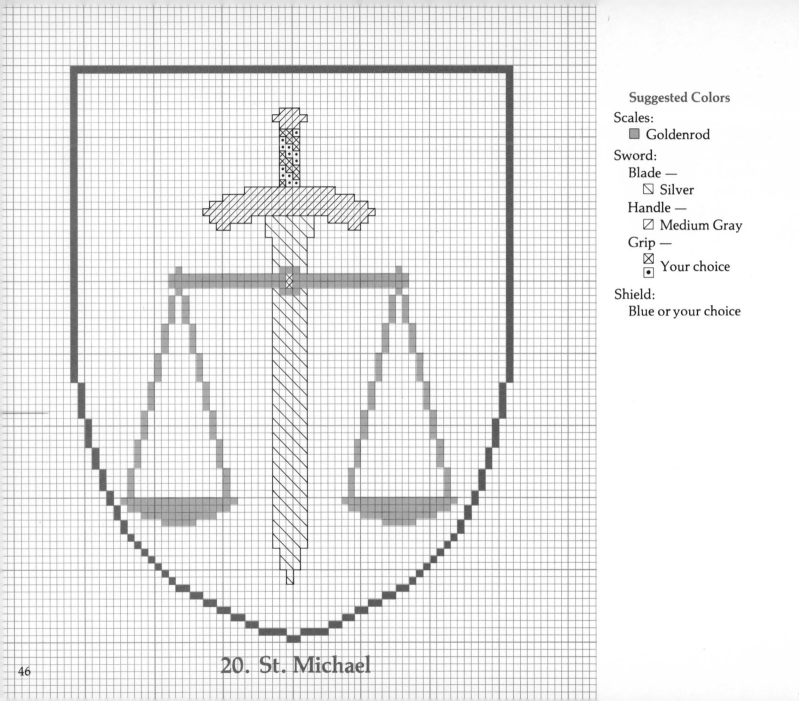

Suggested Colors

Scales:
◼ Goldenrod

Sword:
  Blade —
    ◨ Silver
  Handle —
    ◪ Medium Gray
  Grip —
    ⊠
    ⊡ Your choice

Shield:
  Blue or your choice

20. St. Michael

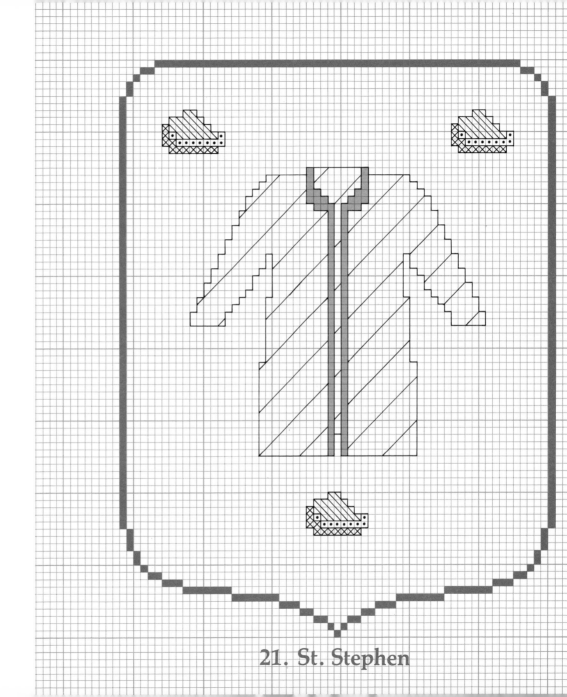

Suggested Colors:

Coat:
- ☑ Regency Gold
- ⬜ Brown

Stones:
- ◩ Silver
- ⊡ Medium Gray
- ⊠ Dark Gray

Shield: Scarlet

Frame: Ivory, White, or your choice.

21. St. Stephen

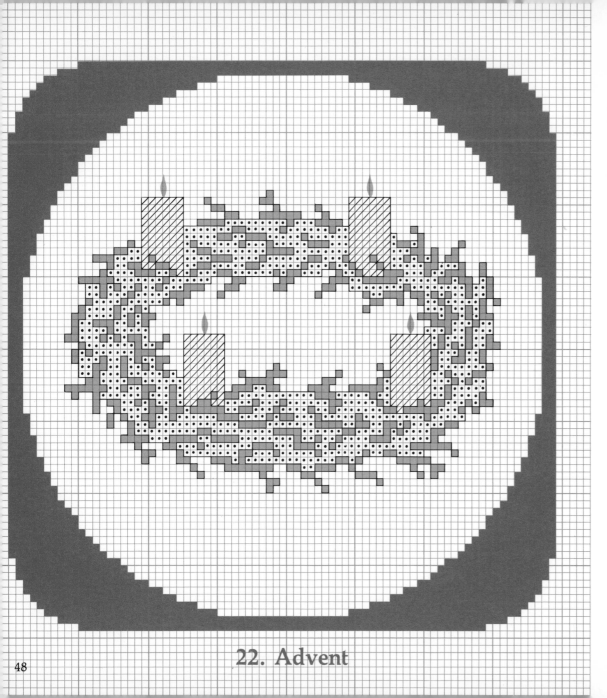

22. Advent

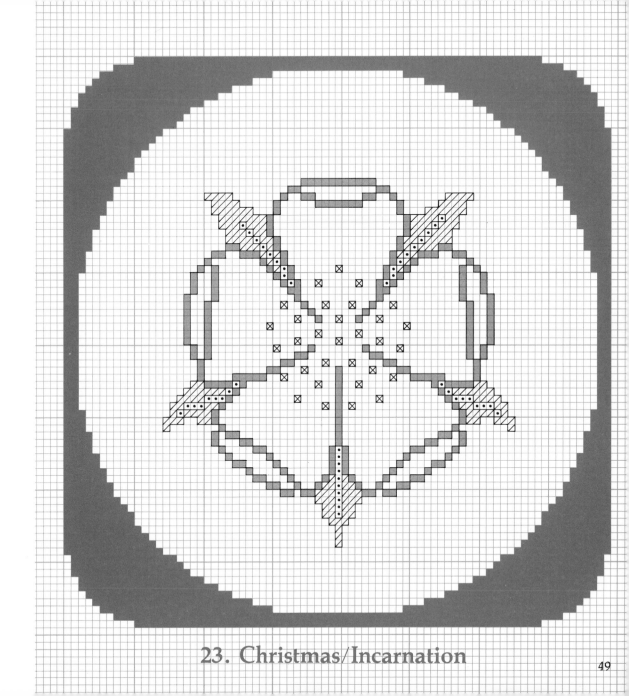

Suggested Colors

Petals:
- ☐ White
- ▧ Regency Gold

Stamens:
- ⊠ Goldenrod

Leaves:
- ⊘ Olive Green
- ⊡ Loden

Frame:
  White or your choice

Background:
  Wedgewood Blue or
  Scarlet

23. Christmas/Incarnation

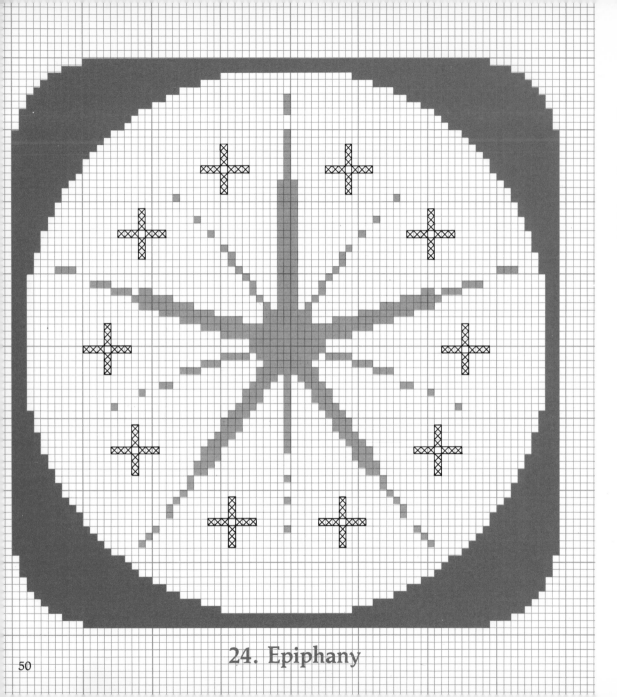

24. Epiphany

Suggested Colors

Star:
⬛ Goldenrod or
    Regency Gold

Crosses:
⊠ Silver

Frame: White

Background: French Blue or
Wedgewood Blue

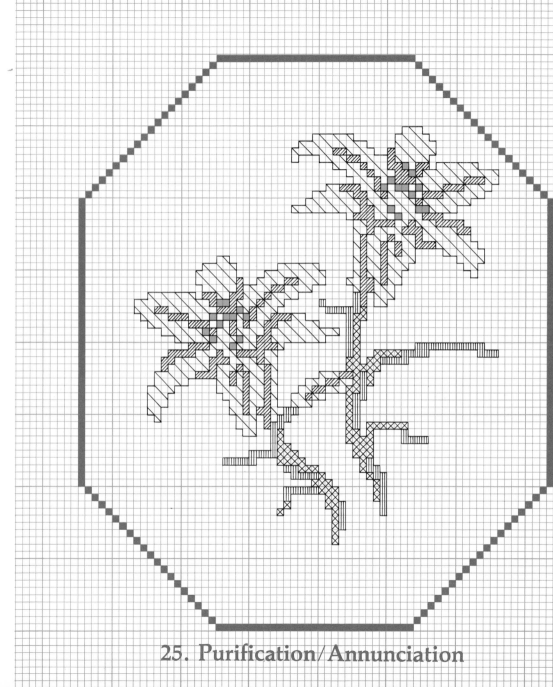

Suggested Colors

Flowers:

    Petals —

        ◳ White

        ◪ Regency Gold

    Stamens —

        ▨ Goldenrod or Orange

    Leaves and Stems —

        ⊠ Loden Green

        ⫴ Olive Green

Border: Goldenrod or
Loden Green

Background: Powder Blue

25. Purification/Annunciation

51

Phoenix:

- ■ Regency Red
- ◪ Scarlet
- □ Gold Nugget
- ⊠ Black
- ⊡ White

Ashes:

- ◸ Medium Gray

Smoke:

- ◪ Silver

Frame: White, or Ivory

26. Easter

Suggested Colors

Chariot:
- ⊠ Deep Red
- ▨ Silver

Wheels:
- □ Black
- ▨ Goldenrod
- □ Very Light Blue

Flames:
- ⊡ Scarlet
- ◨ Orange

Frame:
White or Powder Blue

Background: Very Light Blue

27. Ascension

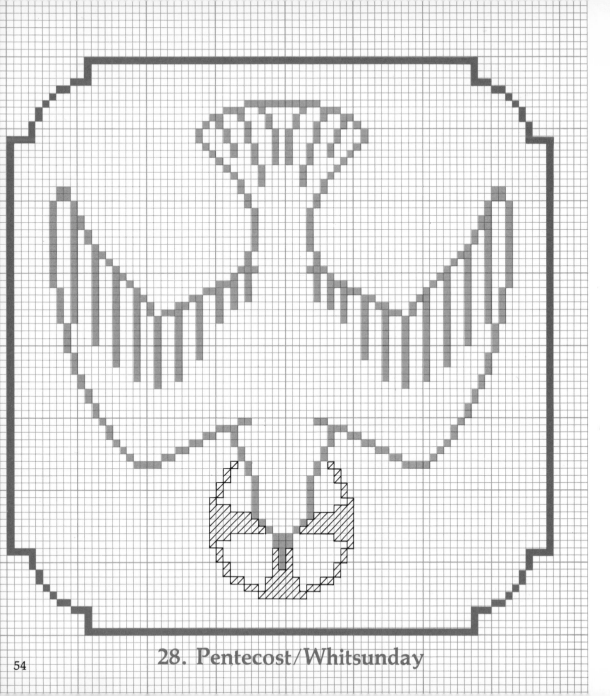

Dove:
- ☐ Snow White
- ☒ Silver

Halo:
- ☑ Goldenrod

Background: Light Blue

Frame: Ivory, White, or
your choice.

28. Pentecost/Whitsunday

Suggested Colors

- ☐ Ivory
- ▨ Goldenrod
- ▨ Green

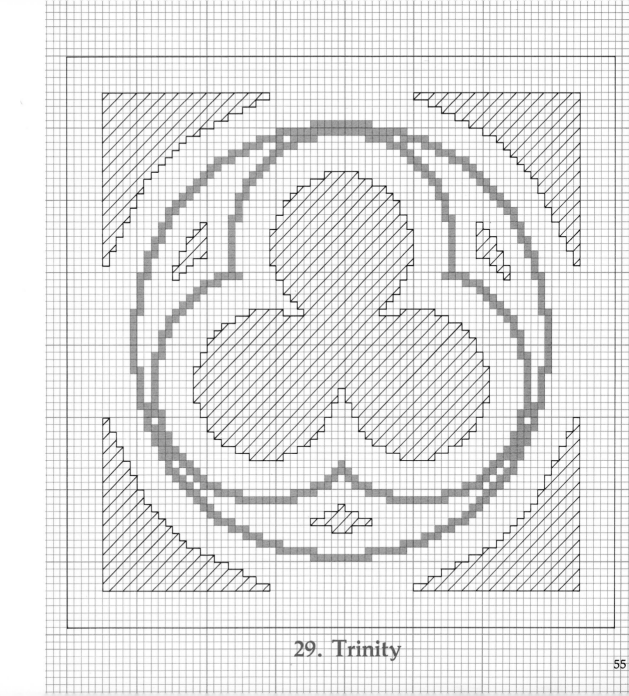

29. Trinity

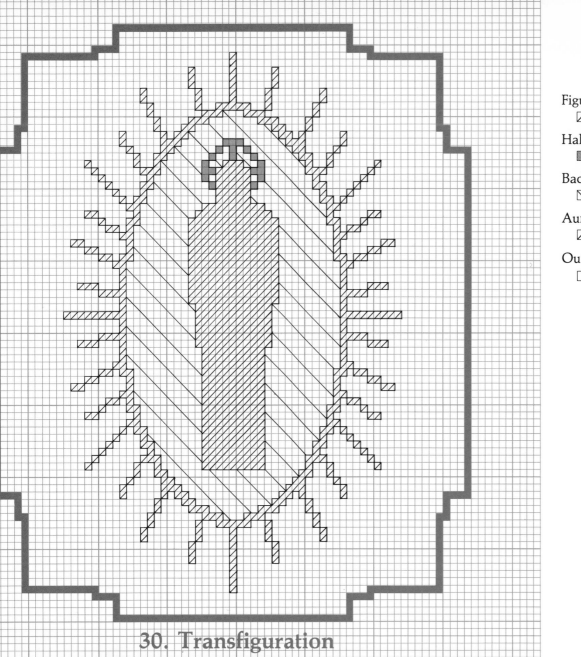

Suggested Colors

Figure:
☑ Glamour White

Halo and Border:
▨ Scarlet

Background to figure:
◨ Goldenrod

Aureole:
☑ Glamour White

Outer background:
☐ Light or Very Light Blue

30. Transfiguration

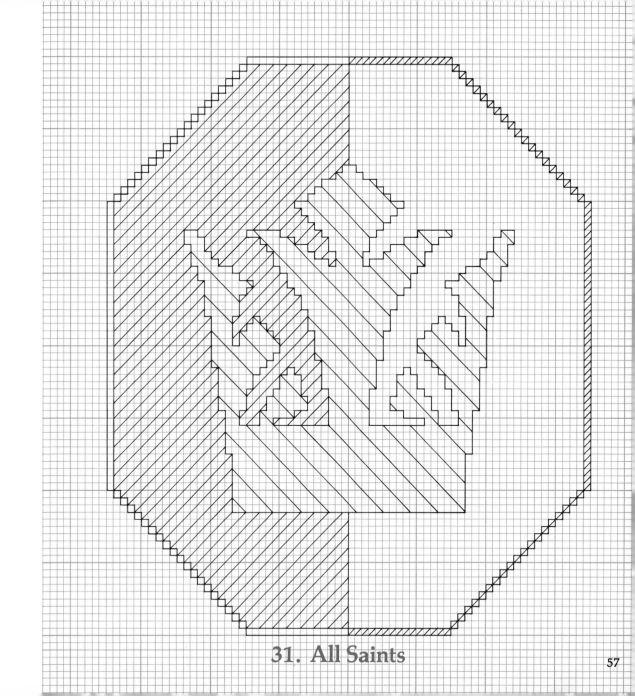

Suggested Colors

Traditional Colors:

Crown:
  ◩ Goldenrod

Frame:
  ☐ ½ Silver
  ◪ ½ Black

Background:
  ◪ ½ Black
  ☐ ½ Silver

31. All Saints

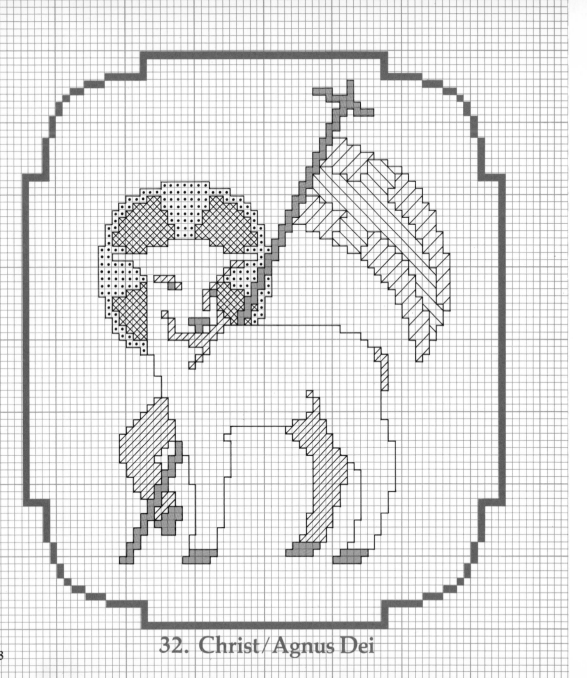

Suggested Colors

Lamb:
  Body and Head:
    □ White
    ☑ Medium Gray
  Eyes, Nose, Hooves —
    ■ Black

Halo:
    ⊡ Goldenrod
    ⊠ Light Yellow

Staff:
    ■ Golden Nugget or
      Light Brown

Banner:
    ◧ Red
    ◨ White

Frame: Goldenrod

Background: Powder Blue

32. Christ/Agnus Dei

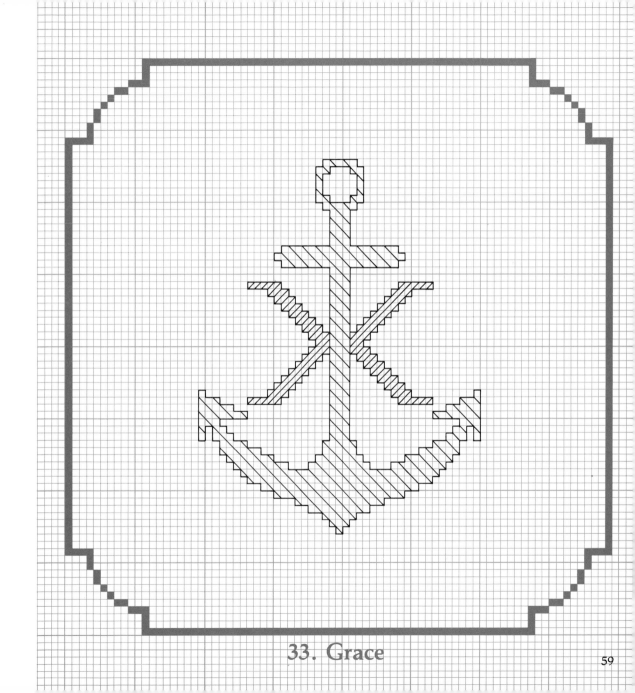

Suggested Colors

Traditional Colors:

Anchor:

◻ Scarlet

Chi (X):

◻ Black

Background: Silver

Frame: Your choice.

33. Grace

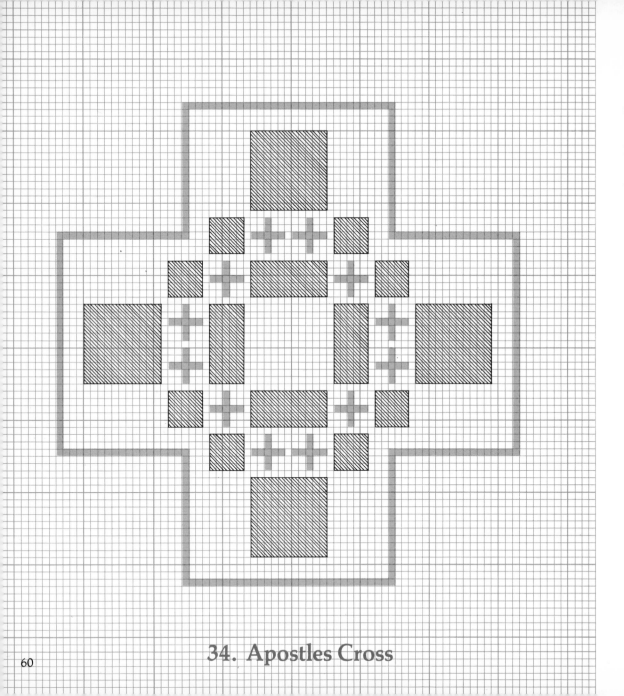

Suggested Colors

Outline and Small Crosses:
▦ Scarlet

Blocks:
◩ Gold Nugget

Background: White

34. Apostles Cross

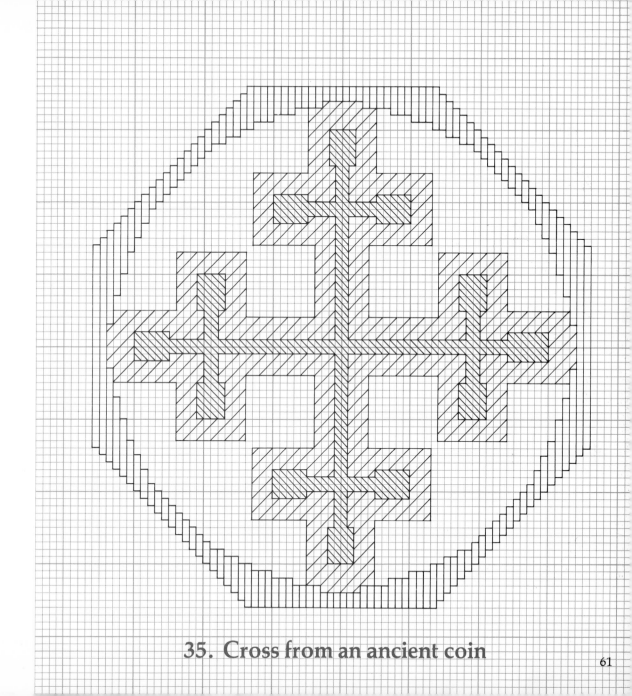

Suggested Colors

Central Cross:
 ◻ Scarlet

Outer part of Cross:
 ◻ Regency Gold

Frame:
 ◻ French Blue

Background: Ivory

35. Cross from an ancient coin

36. Crusaders Cross

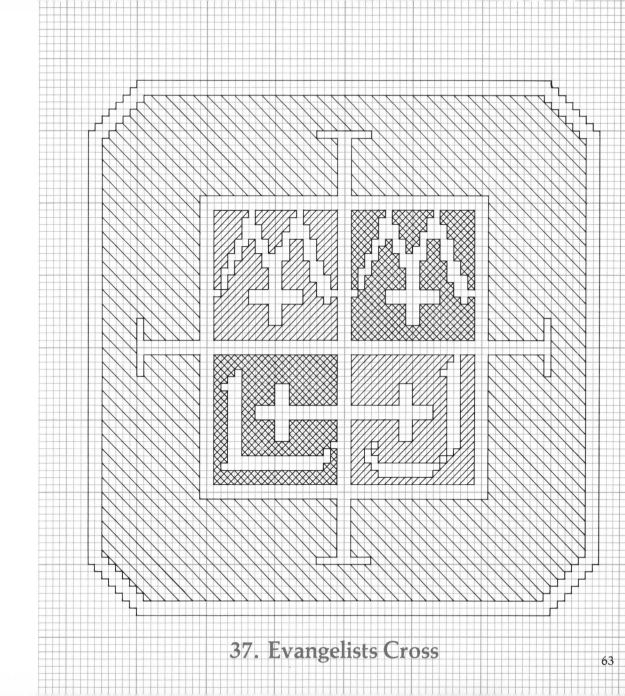

Suggested Colors

Cross, Letters, and Frame:
- ☐ Black
- ☑ Scarlet
- ☒ Azure

Background:
- ◺ Ivory

37. Evangelists Cross

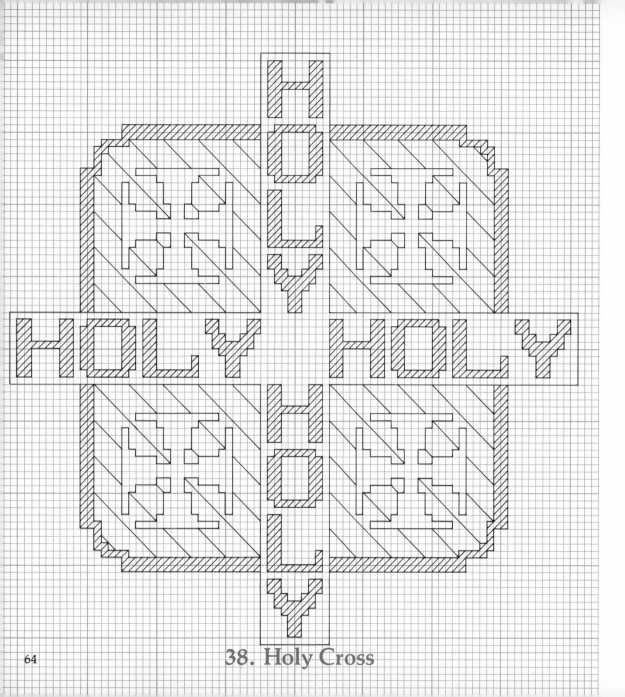

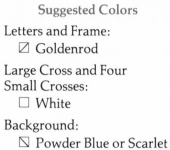

38. Holy Cross

BLOCKING AND MOUNTING

If the correct stitches, *Continental* and *Diagonal Tent,* have been used properly, very little, if any blocking should be necessary. If you have to block, wet thoroughly the needlepoint with cold water and squeeze out the excess with a bath towel; then, using stainless steel rug pins, fasten it all around to a board. Be sure to put the pins into the region of unworked canvas. As you stretch and shape check your measurements and be positive that the piece is squared up accurately (Photo. 1). It will take several days for the needlepoint to dry.

Photo 1

Two ways of mounting will be considered. Both ways apply to pieces with worked sides, as diagrammed at the beginning of the section on *Suggested Layouts,* page 11. One method involves using half-inch plywood in the back and is very firm; the other is semi-soft. In both, foam rubber or styrofoam is used for cushioning. This can be bought from an upholsterer and the best possible quality available should be purchased. The foam should be cut one-half to three-fourths of an inch larger in all directions than the finished needlepoint top. Compression of the foam adds to the resiliency of the cushion. If it is necessary for you to cut the foam, use a sharp razor blade. Hold the foam down with a heavy ruler or board so that the edges will be cut straight.

For both methods of mounting, the corners may be hand sewn from the outside, using matching needlepoint wool as shown in Photo. 2. It is possible, also, to stitch from the inside using button and carpet thread. Care must be taken always to match carefully the needlepoint stitches of the edges at the corners.

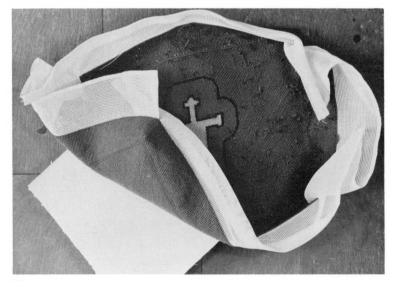

Photo 2

Method A

1. Place the foam inside the cornered canvas and ease, very carefully, into position.

2. Lace the two sides together, using button and carpet thread in a tapestry needle and sewing through the holes of the canvas mesh. Rather than using one very long thread, additional lengths can be tied on as you progress. Pull the thread up to adjust the tension and fasten firmly.

3. Fold and pin short ends and lace them together with more of the thread as shown in Photo. 3.

4. To finish the soft cushion, sew on a fabric back using a strong sewing thread, Photo. 4. Velvet or velveteen is desirable. The fabric you choose should be able to withstand considerable wear.

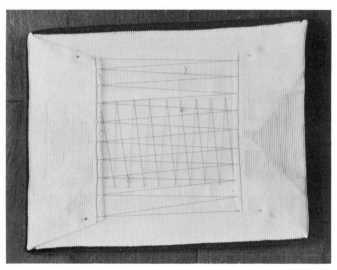

Photo 3

Photo 4

Method B

This method is recommended where there is a rough or uneven slate, or other stone, floor. It involves the use of foam, half-inch plywood, cardboard (or photographer's mat board) and a backing fabric, as shown in Photo. 5. If four rubber feet are added later, the backing fabric may be much less heavy and expensive than the velveteen recommended for Method A.

1. Fit the foam into the cornered canvas.

2. Place the plywood, which has been cut to the exact size of the needlepoint top, on top of the foam.

3. Stretch, smooth, and staple the canvas to the plywood. It is recommended that you start the stapling in the center of each side and then work toward the corners (Photo. 6).

Photo 5

Photo 6

4. Prepare the cardboard, or mat board, by covering it with the cloth which has been cut one inch larger all around. The cloth may be fastened completely to the cardboard using fabric adhesive, or just the edges may be stuck down, taped down, or laced together.

5. The covered cardboard is then sewn to the cushion with needlepoint yarn, matching the stitches to the needlepoint stitches and being sure that the corners fall in exactly the right places.

6. Add four rubber feet and a hanger if desired. These may be purchased in a hardware store (Photo. 7).

Photo 7

These two methods — A and B — apply only to rectangular pieces with attached needlepoint edges. Pieces with tapered or rounded shapes, such as chair seats, should be finished with cording and fabric boxing by one experienced in upholstering.

HELPFUL HINTS

Centering Patterns — Fold canvas in half both ways and mark the center with a safety pin. Note center of pattern (where center heavy lines of graph paper intersect) and start center of pattern at center of canvas.

Canvas — When a canvas is too large to hold conveniently, roll up opposite ends of the canvas to expose only the section to be worked on. Pin or use large flat stainless steel grips to hold the rolled canvas.

Needle Threading — Fold the yarn over and flatten fold by pinching the wool. Then insert the doubled yarn into the needle's eye. Or a small piece of Scotch Tape may be folded over the end of the yarn and this used to thread the wool through the eye.

Yarn — Do not work with yarn that is longer than sixteen to twenty inches. Never knot the yarn, run it under the back side of completed work or hold an inch of wool on the back side and work over it. If the yarn becomes twisted as you work, let go of the threaded needle and allow the yarn to untwist. Work with a light and even tension, being careful not to pull the canvas out of shape. If the work starts to skew, pull the canvas back to square and ease up on your tension. If, in a finished piece of work, there are a few stitches that are too tight, or misplaced, so that the canvas shows through, go over these stitches using half-thickness tapestry yarn or one or two strands of Persian type yarn. When the yarn is down to the last two or three inches, or color is to be changed, weave it through an inch or so of finished work on the back, then clip off closely. Leave no hanging ends to get caught up in the new work. Never reuse yarn that has been ripped out.

Thimbles — can be helpful, as they are in sewing, in pushing needles through the canvas.

As You Work — watch your stitches and consult the pattern carefully. Never let any kind of error stand. Pluck out and correct at once. While later changes are very much harder to make, no mistakes should be allowed to remain in your work.

Cleaning — *Woolite* is excellent for removing stains or dirt from needlepoint. Read and follow the directions on the product.

REFERENCES

Agnew, Patience. *Needlepoint for Churches.* New York: Charles Scribner's Sons, 1972.

Griffith, Helen Stuart. *Sign Language of Our Faith.* Grand Rapids: Wm. B. Eerdmans Publishing Co., 1966.

*Matheus, Wendell. *Basic Symbols of the Church.* Philadelphia: Fortress Press, 1971.

Post, W. Ellwood. *Saints, Signs and Symbols.* New York: Morehouse-Barlow Co., rev. ed., 1974.

*Rest, Friedrich. *Our Christian Symbols.* Philadelphia: The Christian Education Press, 1954.

*Roeder, Helen. *Saints and Their Attributes.* Chicago: Henry Regnery Co., 1956.

Thompson, David W. *Symbols of the Church.* Needham Heights: Whittemore Associates, 1973.

*Troyer, Johannes. *The Cross as Symbol and Ornament.* Philadelphia: The Westminister Press, 1961.

*Out of print, but may be available in church or public libraries.

Symbols of the Church — a series of six color/sound filmstrips — would make good background to see before starting a Church Needlepoint project. Individual strips cover Symbols of the Faith, Symbols of the Cross, Symbols of the House of God, Symbols of the Old Testament, Symbols of the New Testament, and the Lost Symbols. This series may be obtained from denominational bookstores or from Cathedral Films, 2921 W. Alameda Ave., Box 1608, Burbank, California 91505.

APPENDIX I

Steps involved in transforming a book illustration to a piece of complete needlepoint.

1. *Grace* symbol — the anchor and the Greek letter X (chi) as it appears in Post's *Saints, Signs, and Symbols* 2nd edition, page 79. The shield in that book is actually two and three eighths inches high.

2. The symbol enlarged to the desired size. In this case the chosen size is about five and one quarter inches high. It was chosen to fit within the shield shape selected for certain of the St. Paul's Cathedral kneelers. An exact replica of the symbol in Post was not wanted so the pattern was both modified and simplified as it was drawn on to the ten squares to the inch graph paper. Notice that some account was taken of the squares, in placing the diagram. Actually, you would never make as finished a drawing as this. Just a light sketch would be made and then the pattern converted directly to stitches on the same paper.

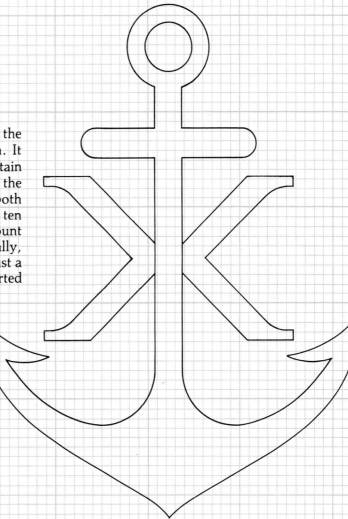

3. The diagram converted to stitches. Neither the anchor nor the X will have an outline, but to make these two parts of the symbol distinguishable two colors will be used. Where slanted and curved lines must appear in a needlepoint pattern, great care must be taken in working out the "steps" which replace them.

THREE. Legends for steps involved in transforming a book diagram to finished needle-point. *Note* that the three diagrams should be reduced by the same amount and the transparency enlarged so the symbol will be of comparable size.

4. The pattern worked into needlepoint. Scarlet and silver were selected for the Grace symbol, a sapphire shield and a silver shield outline. Note how well the shield outline stands out between the sapphire and the avocado. Color selection is always very important.